How do I feel about

MAKING

FRIENDS

Sarah Levete

COPPER BEECH BOOKS • BROOKFIELD, CONNECTICUT

© Aladdin Books Ltd 1996
© U.S. text 1998

Designed and produced by
Aladdin Books Ltd
28 Percy Street
London W1P 0LD

First published in the United States
in 1998 by
Copper Beech Books,
an imprint of
The Millbrook Press
2 Old New Milford Road
Brookfield, Connecticut 06804

Printed in Belgium
5 4 3 2 1

Designer   Tessa Barwick
Editor   Jen Green
Illustrator   Christopher O'Neill
Photographer   Roger Vlitos

**Library of Congress
Cataloging-in-Publication Data**
Levete, Sarah.
Making Friends / Sarah Levete.
p. cm. — (How do I feel about)
Originally published: Loneliness and making
friends. London: Franklin Watts, 1996.
Summary: Discusses the importance of
friendships, from making friends to resolving
disagreements, and how to deal with feelings
such as jealousy, shyness, and rejection.
Supt. of Docs. no. 158.2/5
ISBN 0-7613-0808-3 (lib. bdg.)
1. Friendship—Juvenile literature.
2. Loneliness— Juvenile literature.
[1. Friendship.] I. Title. II. Series.
BF575.F66L48 1998 97-41646
CIP AC

Contents

Introduction

Kev, Amy, Josh, and Elly are friends. Friends trust each other and have fun together. Sometimes it's nice to be by yourself. At other times if you are alone, but want to be with others, you may feel lonely. The four friends will share their ideas on making friends and the ups and downs of friendships.

Feeling Lonely

Amy and Kev talked when their class went swimming.
Amy has just moved to the area. She is telling Kev that she
sometimes feels lonely because she doesn't know many people.
There are lots of reasons why a person may feel lonely.
Have you ever felt lonely?

It can be great to be alone...

...but it can also feel lonely.

▶ It's OK To Be Alone

Being alone does not mean you are lonely. It can be fun to watch a TV program or read a book all by yourself.

At other times, if you want to talk to a friend and there is nobody there, then you may feel lonely.

▼ Do They Like Me?

Sometimes it can seem as if everyone except for you has lots of friends. That can make you feel lonely, and a bit jealous too. Feeling lonely can make you nervous about making new friends.

◀ The Same, But Different!

From our heads to our toes, we are all different. But whether you are big or small, or your skin is black or white, we are all people who deserve friendship and respect. It can feel lonely if someone is unkind, or leaves you out because you are different from them. People who do this miss out on good friendships.

1. Chaz's dad gave him a game for his birthday. But he had no one to play with.

2. Chaz hoped his new game would help him to make friends at school.

3. Chaz shouted at his dad because the game hadn't made Chaz any friends.

Why was Chaz mad at his dad?

Chaz felt lonely and angry. He took his feelings out on his dad. That wasn't very fair. It wasn't his dad's fault that Chaz found it difficult to make friends.

Feeling lonely can make you act angrily toward the people who care about you.

It would have made Chaz feel better if he had told his dad how he felt.

▼ I Don't Care . . .

Sometimes feeling lonely can make you feel nasty. You may think that there is no point in being nice to others because you don't have any friends anyway. But being mean will only make you feel more lonely and unhappy.

Why don't you want to go to school?

◄ I'm Scared

Feeling lonely can make you feel less confident. You may not want to go to school because being with lots of other people can make you feel even more alone.

If someone is friendly, you may feel too shy to be friendly back.

This will teach them not to ignore me.

Amy, how did it feel when you were lonely?

"I felt as if nobody would ever like me. I thought I would never have anyone to play with.

When we moved here, I missed my old friends. Everybody at my new school already knew each other, and they all seemed to have friends. I was angry at my mom for making us move here. But after awhile I began to feel more at home and then I made friends with Elly."

7

Why Friends Are Important

Josh and Elly are talking about why friends are important to them. Josh enjoys having lots of friends because he can do different things with them. Elly likes being able to tell her friends jokes, even if they don't laugh at them!

Why are friends important to you?

I like skating with some friends and swapping books with others.

I can tell friends things that I can't tell other people.

Friends can trust each other.

8

Friends make some things easier!

▼ Good Times

Have you ever been told a really funny joke and wanted to tell someone else, to make them laugh?

You can share good times with friends. You can have a laugh, even if they tell rotten jokes!

Don't worry. I'll help you.

I'll never be able to do this.

◀ Bad Times

If you've had a difficult day at school or had a fight with your mom or dad, it can really help to talk things over with a friend.

A friend can't make a bad day go away, but it certainly helps to talk.

I've been dying to tell you this all day!

Elly, what do friends mean to you?

"I have a few good friends who matter to me a lot. We can be honest with each other about how we feel. You can talk to friends when you're angry and know that they will understand. Friends are people you trust and who make you feel safe and happy. Mom and dad are my friends too."

9

Making Friends

Elly and Amy are now good friends, though it took Amy a long time to believe anyone would like her. There are lots of different ways to make friends but it's important to remember that friends are people you can trust. People who make you feel uncomfortable are not friends. If you feel unsure about someone, tell a grown-up.

Friends don't make threats.

Making friends can be easy!

▶ Who Will Notice Me?

Sometimes it seems as if everyone else is always saying something funny or clever, or has better games to play than you.

Don't worry. Everyone feels like that sometimes. In fact, everyone else is probably feeling the same as you!

▼ Sing And Dance!

Have you ever thought of joining a club or a group? It's a great way to meet people. You may feel shy at first, but others probably feel the same.

Making friends can be fun — so why not make a song and dance about it?

◀ Silent Friends

A cat or dog can be your friend. So can an imaginary friend that no one else can see.

But it's also important to have "real" friends of your own age, who you can chat with and do things with. Real friends can also cheer you up if you feel sad.

1. Jo wanted to make friends. She tried pushing in, but the others ignored her.

2. Jo gave her candy away to try and make friends. It didn't work.

3. Jo asked Susie to play. Susie said yes. Jo and Susie became friends.

Jo found it hard to make friends.

There is no magic recipe for making friends. Sometimes it can be easy, but at other times it can feel like very hard work.

As Jo discovered, pushing in doesn't work — it's not very friendly. "Buying" friends doesn't work, either. What happens when you run out of candy? The best way to make friends is to be friendly, and to be yourself!

▼ Does It Feel OK?

Nobody should offer you presents to make friends with you. People who make threats aren't really friends, either. If a person threatens you or makes you feel uneasy, or says your friendship must be a secret, tell a grown-up you trust.

Would you like to play?

◄ Help Make It Easy

If you see someone who looks a bit lost and alone, why not ask him or her to join in with your friends? It may not make much difference to you, but it may make someone else feel really happy.

Let's be friends. I'll buy you that candy.

Amy, do you make friends easily?

"Not really. Sometimes I think that nobody will like me — that makes me feel shy. Even though I don't always feel like it, I make an extra effort to be friendly at school. It makes it easier when other people make an effort to include me too. Jan asked me to play and now we're friends.

But I wouldn't be friends if someone offered me presents or made threats. I'd tell my mom."

13

Different Friendships

Elly is reading Josh a really funny part from a letter from her friend Ben who lives far away. Elly doesn't see Ben very often but they write to each other. There are lots of different kinds of friendships, from best friends to groups of friends. Can you think of any other kinds of friendships?

He sounds really nice.

Super! He's coming to stay!

Groups of friends are fun.

14

Try writing to a friend.

▼ Friends Feel Good!

You may be surprised to realize that your mom, dad, brother, or sister is actually a lot of fun as a friend, too.

There are no rules about who you can be friends with, as long as they make you feel good and comfortable.

◄ Best Friends

Some people have several friends, but one *best* friend. This is often the person they feel closest to.

It's great having a best friend, but don't worry if you don't have one. All kinds of friends are equally important.

Josh, tell us about your friends.

"I have lots of different friends. My sister is a good friend, even though I get angry with her when she beats me at football.

My best friend is Toby. We tell each other everything — but I'm not telling you what we say!

Sometimes I go around in a group and do things with lots of friends — that's fun, too."

Difficult Times

Josh is telling Kev that he is angry with his best friend, Toby, because Toby went off and played with someone else. Sometimes even best friends like Josh and Toby have arguments. Being friends with someone isn't always easy. Can you think of reasons why being friends can be difficult?

Friendships can be hard.

16

Arguments don't last forever.

It's not fair. He gets everything he wants.

◀ *Feeling Jealous*

You may feel jealous of a friend because he or she has something you want, or has been invited to a party instead of you.

But part of being a friend is enjoying someone else's good luck, however difficult that is!

▶ *Don't Worry!*

If you have been left out of a game or not invited to someone's party, you will know that it can make you feel angry and lonely.

Remember, it happens to everyone. It doesn't mean that no one likes you or you will never be included.

Why hasn't anyone chosen me?

▲ *What's Gone Wrong?*

It is upsetting when a person you like or feel close to suddenly doesn't want to be your friend. You may not understand why. But friendships do change over time, and we all have to accept that, although it's hard.

1. Penny and Ashika were best friends. They walked to school together.

2. They met another friend of Penny's named Anne. Ashika looked angry.

3. Ashika didn't want Penny to have other friends.

Why was Ashika angry?

Ashika didn't think that Penny could be friends with both Anne and her. But Ashika might have liked Anne if she had given her more of a chance.

Sometimes you may feel jealous of the other people your friend likes. But just because a person has more than one friend, it doesn't mean that they like you any less, or that you are less special to them.

18

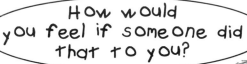

brief## ▼ Say NO!

If a friend dares you to do something that you feel is wrong, don't do it — even if he or she makes fun of you. So-called friends like that aren't worth it. It's better to lose a friend than to do something you know is wrong.

Difficult Times

◀ Speak Up

No one has the right to hurt someone else or make anyone feel unhappy.

If you see a friend being unkind to someone, explain why you feel what they did was wrong. Friends can be wrong sometimes!

Kev, have you had problems with friends?

"I hung around with a group who started stealing. They told me to keep it a secret, but I didn't want to join in. I talked to my dad and decided to leave the group. I'm glad I did. Secrets are great, but there are some secrets that friends shouldn't ask you to keep. If it feels wrong, say NO."

19

Working At Friendships

Kev and Elly are at Josh's birthday party. Josh and his friend Toby have made up — they are best friends again! Kev and Elly know that friends can have good and bad times. Being honest about how you feel can save a friendship. Can you think of other ways to work at friendships?

Friends have to let you be by yourself sometimes.

No thanks. I want to read my book!

If I get angry with a friend it helps if we talk about it.

▼ Try Talking!

If you and a friend have an argument or get angry, talk to each other about how you feel. If you still feel angry with each other, you might ask your mom or dad to sit with you both so you can sort it out.

She's great, isn't she?

I think I understand.

◄ Make Space!

It's important to think about other people's feelings. Sometimes you may be the center of attention, and at other times you won't. But remember, there's lots of time for everyone.

Elly, what are your tips for staying good friends?

"I think that it is important to tell a friend what you are thinking — even if you are really angry with the person.

Unless you can say sorry and forgive each other, you might stay angry forever. Friends are special — try not to lose them!"

Don't Forget . . .

Josh, what do friends mean to you?

"A friend is someone you can be yourself with, even if you are sad or angry. You can have a laugh with a friend. But sometimes you have to say you're sorry, like I did with Toby. Because he's my friend, he didn't stay angry at me — we even joked about it, later."

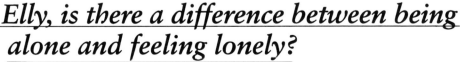

Elly, is there a difference between being alone and feeling lonely?

"Yes. When you are by yourself and feel good about it, that's not feeling lonely. eeling lonely is when you want to be with a friend, but there is nobody there.
I felt lonely when my friend Ben moved away — I really missed talking to him. I found it hard to make new friends."

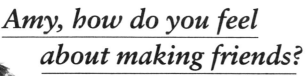

Amy, how do you feel about making friends?

"I still feel a bit shy and nervous about making friends, but I try to make an effort to be friendly.

Elly persuaded me to try for a part in the school play — I met some really nice people there. I think we were all nervous, but once we got talking it was fun. I got a part, too!"

LINE FOR PARTS IN THE SCHOOL PLAY

Kev, can you make sure no one feels lonely?

"Not really, but you can try to make everyone feel welcome, especially if they are new to a group. Not everyone finds it easy to make friends. Even if you don't want to be best friends with someone, there's no harm in being nice to them."

Index

All the photographs in this book have been posed by models. The publishers would like to thank them all.